Hello!
I am dangerous.

I0115134

DANGER in the animal kingdom means something that can hurt or cause problems. Some animals can use their teeth or venom to protect themselves. Others might use their size and get upset if they feel threatened.

WARNING!

The animals shown in this book are extremely dangerous! If you find yourself in the wild or an area where one of these animals calls home, be very careful and avoid them at all costs.

Saltwater Crocodile

DANGER: Large, aggressive predator with a powerful bite

I sneak up slowly on my prey, and attack in the water or on land.

Saltwater crocodiles have an incredible sense of smell. It helps them to easily find their prey.

Poison Dart Frog

DANGER: Makes strong toxin from its skin

My vibrant colors let everyone know that I am dangerous.

Poison dart frogs become toxic by eating special tiny bugs in the wild.

African Elephant

DANGER: Huge size and strength

When an elephant feels threatened they can "charge" and trample anything in thier way.

Sometimes I do a fake charge, just to scare you away.

Stonefish

DANGER: Master of disguise with poison spikes on its back

Stonefish are well-hidden on the ocean floor, waiting for prey to approach.

Lion

DANGER: Powerful strength and amazing hunting abilities

Lions are the only big cats that are social. They have close lion friends and live in groups called "prides".

You tell 'em!

Lions are excellent predators and can take down prey much larger than themselves.

Cassowary

DANGER: Powerful legs with sharp claws

With just three toes on each foot cassowaries slice enemies with dangerous kicks.

Don't you think the "casque" on the top of my head is cool?

They are excellent swimmers and can cross rivers and creeks.

Komodo Dragon

DANGER: Powerful bite and saliva that has harmful bacteria

The bacteria in their spit doesn't let their prey's blood clot, so it keeps bleeding.

My dirty mouth helps me hunt.

Komodo dragons are the largest lizards on Earth.

Bullet Ant

DANGER: Intense pain from its sting

I have the most painful sting of any insect.

Scientists study bullet ants to learn more about helping people with pain.

The pain from a bullet ant sting can last for over 24 hours.

Jellyfish

DANGER: One of the most powerful animal toxins

Cobra

DANGER: Big bite and venom that can stop its prey's from breathing

I can "hood up" to look bigger and more dangerous.

Some species of cobras can spit their venom at a target.

Hippopotamus

DANGER: Aggressive behavior, especially near the water

A hippo's big teeth can grow up to 20 inches (51cm) long.

My bite is strong enough to crush bones.

Coral Snake

DANGER: Powerful venom that attacks the brain

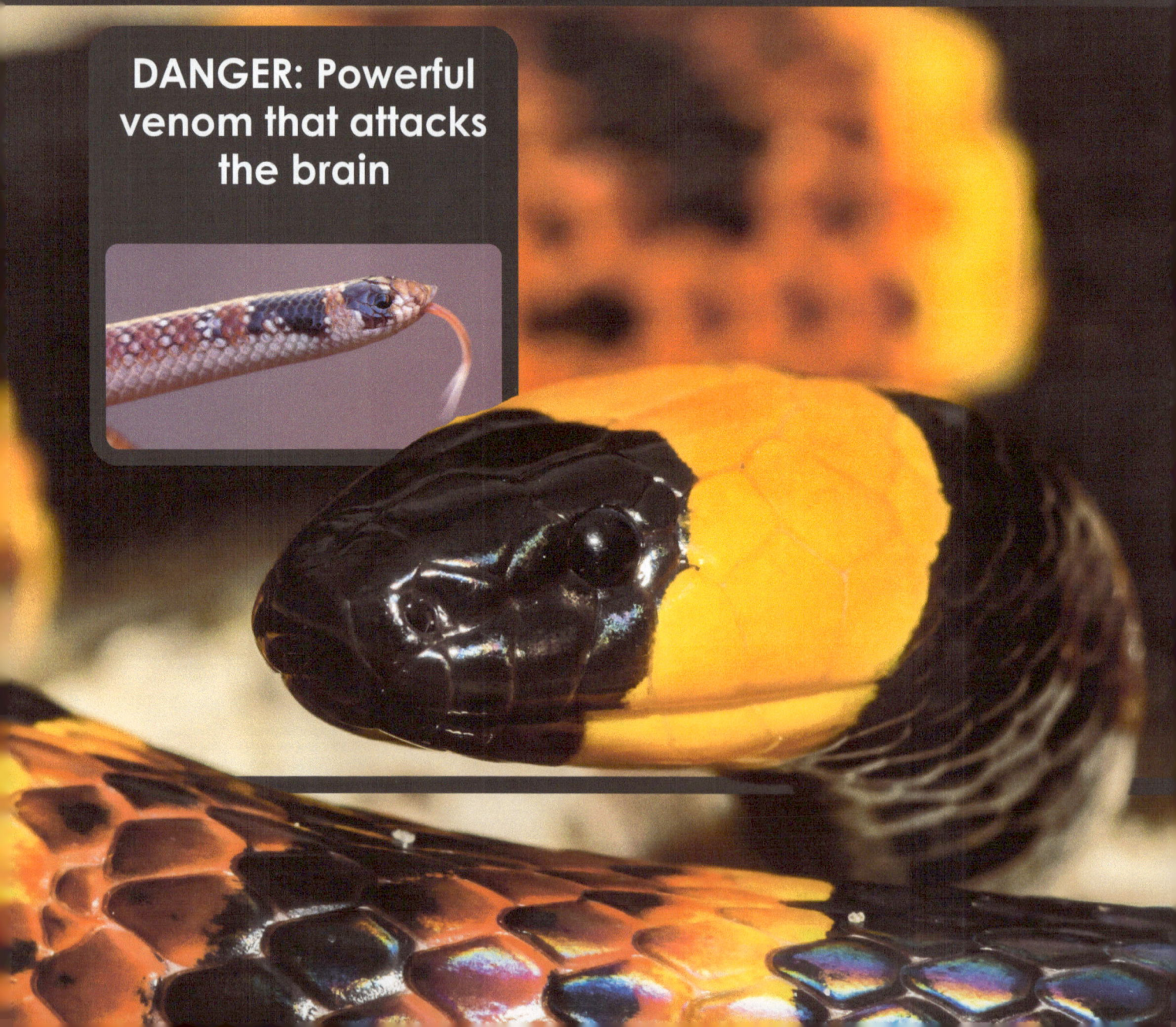

Pufferfish

DANGER: Contains "tetrodotoxin", a strong poison that attacks the brain and nerves

Pufferfish often have spines that become more "spiky" when they "puff" up.

Cape Buffalo

DANGER: Big body, unpredictable behavior, and sharp horns

Cape buffalos have few predators beacause the are so big and strong.

I often attack without warning!

Cape buffalos are especially dangerous at night.

Gila Monster

DANGER:
Venomous bite

Gila monsters are usually slow-moving lizards, but they can be surprisingly quick when they want to be.

They say my bite is super painful.

Once a gila monster bites, it will often hold on to its prey for a very long time.

Want more?

... and more

Hello parents!

Visit us to find out about new releases and **FREE** offers. We'll let you know when we have a new release coming out and how you can get it for FREE.

And you can cast your vote for what book we make next!

scan here

ActiveBrainsBooks.com

or visit here

---

scan here

Let us know what you think. As an independent publisher, your honest reviews mean a lot to us and our business. We'd love to hear from you!

amazon.com/review/create-review/

or visit here

FOLLOW US on Amazon.

amazon.com/author/activebrainsbooks

ActiveBrainsBooks.com

ACTIVE BRAINS

www.ingramcontent.com/pod-product-compliance
Lightning Source LLC
Chambersburg PA
CBHW060843270326
41933CB00003B/185